First World War
and Army of Occupation
War Diary
France, Belgium and Germany

60 DIVISION
181 Infantry Brigade
London Regiment
2/23 Battalion
4 November 1915 - 31 December 1915

WO95/3032/6

Published by

The Naval & Military Press Ltd

Unit 10 Ridgewood Industrial Park,

Uckfield, East Sussex,

TN22 5QE England

Tel: +44 (0) 1825 749494

www.naval-military-press.com

www.nmarchive.com

This diary has been reprinted in facsimile from the original. Any imperfections are inevitably reproduced and the quality may fall short of modern type and cartographic standards.

© Crown Copyright
Images reproduced by permission of The National Archives, London, England, 2015.

Contents

Document type	Place/Title	Date From	Date To
Heading	WO95/3032/6		
Heading	60 Division 181 Brigade 2/23 London Regt 1915 Sep-1915 Dec		
Miscellaneous	Unit 2/23rd Battalion The London Regiment	04/09/1915	04/09/1915
War Diary	Hockerill Camp Bishops Stortford		
War Diary	Braintree	04/11/1915	30/11/1915
War Diary	Braintree	04/11/1915	04/11/1915
Heading	War-Diary Of 2/23rd Battalion London Regiment December 1st-31st 1915		
War Diary	Braintree	01/12/1915	31/12/1915
Miscellaneous	Tactical Exercise	31/12/1915	31/12/1915
Miscellaneous	Operation Orders By Lieut-Colonel H. Streatfeild Commanding 2/23rd Battalion The London Regiment	03/12/1915	03/12/1915
Miscellaneous	General Idea		
Miscellaneous	Instructions		
Miscellaneous	Tactical Exercise 2/23rd Battalion The London Regiment	17/12/1915	17/12/1915
Miscellaneous	Operation Orders By Lieut-Colonel H. Streatfeild Commanding 2/23rd Battalion The London Regiment Braintree	17/12/1915	17/12/1915
Miscellaneous	General Idea		
Miscellaneous	Tactical Exercise 2/23rd Battalion The London Regiment	31/12/1915	31/12/1915
Miscellaneous	Orders By Lieut-Colonel H. Streatfeild Commanding 2/23rd Battalion The London Regiment	30/12/1915	30/12/1915
Miscellaneous	General Idea		

WO 95/3032/6

60 DIVISION

181 BRIGADE

2/23 LONDON REGT

1915 SEP — 1915 DEC

2904

Unit. 2/23rd. Battalion. The London Regiment.

Brigade. 181st. Infantry Brigade.

Division. 60th. London Division.

Mobilisation Centre.-------------

Temporary War Station. Hockerill Camp, Bishops Stortford. Herts.

Stations since occupied subsequent to) Clapham Junction.
concentration.   ) White City.
                                         Horley.
                                         Hatfield.
                                         Bishops Stortford.
                                         Hockerill Camp.

(a) Mobilisation..............

(b) Concentration at War Station: (Including Railway moves)......

(c) Organisation for Defence: (Including vulnerable points).......

(d) Training: Progressing favourably. Unit now employed on Musketry, Physical Training, Bayonet Fighting and Field Work. Standard of Shooting is good.

(e) Discipline: Very good.

(f) Administration:

    (1) Medical Services: Since moving under canvas a R.A.M.C Doctor has been attached for duty.

    (2) Veterinary Services: Very good.

    (3) Supply Services: Good.

    (4) Transport Services: Satisfactory.

    (5) Ordnance Services: Satisfactory.

    (6) Billeting and Hutting: None.

    (7) Channel of Correspondence in Routine Matters.........

    (8) Range Construction: Satisfactory.

    (9) Supply of remounts: Satisfactory.

(g) Re-organisation of T.F. into Home & Imperial Services........

(h) Preparation of Units for Imperial Service:..................

..................Major.
for O.C. 2/23rd. Battn. London Regt.

Hockerill Camp.
4-9-15.

Army Form C. 2118.

WAR DIARY
or
INTELLIGENCE SUMMARY.
(Erase heading not required.)

2/20 London
2/25-th Battalion The London Regt.

Instructions regarding War Diaries and Intelligence Summaries are contained in F.S. Regs., Part II. and the Staff Manual respectively. Title pages will be prepared in manuscript.

Hour, Date, Place	Summary of Events and Information	Remarks and references to Appendices
	Nothing to report.	

2/25... Major

Army Form C. 2118.

WAR DIARY
or
INTELLIGENCE SUMMARY.
(Erase heading not required.)

2/23rd Battalion, The London Regiment.

Hour, Date, Place	Summary of Events and Information	Remarks and references to Appendices
Braintree. 4th December 1915.		
1st November 1915	Marched from Hockerill Camp to billets at Braintree. Weather very wet.	
2nd -do-	Nothing to report	
3rd -do-	Nothing to report	
4th -do-	Nothing to report	
5th -do-	Lieutenant & Quartermaster W.W.Allsopp proceeded to 1/23rd Battalion The London Regiment with British Expeditionary Force. Major V. Dicks joined for duty from 3rd Line.	
6th -do-	Nothing to report	
7th -do-	Nothing to report	
8th -do-	Nothing to report	
9th -do-	Nothing to report	
10th -do-	Nothing to report	
11th -do-	Nothing to report	
12th -do-	Nothing to report	
13th -do-	Nothing to report	
14th -do-	Nothing to report	

Army Form C. 2118.

Sheet 2.

WAR DIARY
or
INTELLIGENCE SUMMARY.
(*Erase heading not required.*)

2/23rd Battalion The London Regiment.

Hour, Date, Place	Summary of Events and Information	Remarks and references to Appendices
15th November 1915	Received from C.O.O. Weedon 525 .303 Rifles. Received from C.O.O. Weedon 157,920 rounds .303 Ammunition. Handed over to A.S.C. 8 Limbered Wagons Received in exchange 8 G.S. Wagons.	
16th —do—	Handed over 513 Japanese Rifles to C.O.O. Weedon. Handed over 127,000 rounds Japanese Ammunition to C.O.O. Weedon.	
17th —do—	Nothing to report	
18th —do—	Nothing to report	
19th —do—	Nothing to report	
20th —do—	Nothing to report	
21st —do—	Nothing to report	
22nd —do—	Nothing to report	
23rd —do—	Nothing to report	
24th —do—	Nothing to report	
25th —do—	Handed over 12 Japanese Rifles to C.O.O. Weedon Handed over 23 rounds Japanese Ammunition.	
26th —do—	Nothing to report	
27th —do—	Nothing to report	
28th —do—	Nothing to report	
29th —do—	Nothing to report	
30th —do—	Nothing to report	

Lieut. Colonel
Commanding 2/23rd Battalion The London Regiment.

Army Form C. 2118.

WAR DIARY
or
INTELLIGENCE SUMMARY.
(Erase heading not required.)

2/23rd Battalion, The London Regiment.

ORDERLY ROOM - 4 OCT 1915 2nd LINE 23rd LONDON R.

Hour, Date, Place	Summary of Events and Information	Remarks and references to Appendices
Braintree. 4/11/1915.	On October 16th 1915, Lieut. Colonel H.Streatfeild of the 1/23rd Battalion, The London Regiment, British Expeditionary Force took over the command of this Battalion vice Lieut. Colonel F.Kayser transfered to 3/23rd Battalion, The London Regiment. On November 1st. 1915 this Battalion moved from Hockerill Camp into billets at Braintree.	

.... Lieut. Colonel.
Commanding 2/23rd Bn. London Regt.

Instructions regarding War Diaries and Intelligence Summaries are contained in F.S. Regs., Part II. and the Staff Manual respectively. Title pages will be prepared in manuscript.

CONFIDENTIAL
WAR — DIARY of
2/23rd Battalion London Regiment
December 1st – 31st – 1915.

Army Form C. 2118.

WAR DIARY

2/23rd Battalion London Regiment.

(Erase heading not required.)

Instructions regarding War Diaries and Intelligence Summaries are contained in F.S. Regs., Part II. and the Staff Manual respectively. Title pages will be prepared in manuscript.

Hour, Date, Place	Summary of Events and Information	Remarks and references to Appendices
BRAINTREE. 1/12/15	Adjutants Parade 8-30 A.M. — Company Training.	J.B.J.
" 2/12/15.	Brigade Tactical Scheme. 9.45 A.M. to 4 P.M.	J.B.J.
" 3/12/15.	Capt. E.S. MARKS returned to duty from 181st Infantry Bde.	J.B.J.
" 4/12/15.	Outpost Scheme. Interior Economy and Kit inspection.	J.B.J. See Appendix I
" 5/12/15.	Church Parade.	J.B.J.
" 6/12/15.	Company Training.	J.B.J.
" 7/12/15.	Company Training.	J.B.J.
" 8/12/15.	Capt. A.H. CRABBE and 2nd Lt. W.A.S. COTTON transferred to 3/23rd Batt. London Regiment. Capt. H.B. FOX granted 7 days Sick Leave. Capt. P.H. CHEEK (Transport Officer) granted Sick leave until further notice to undergo operation. Batt. Route March, circular via BLACK NOTLEY, YOUNGS END returning via RAYNE 8/30 A.M. till 3 P.M.	J.B.J. J.G.

Army Form C. 2118.

WAR DIARY
or
INTELLIGENCE SUMMARY. 2/23 Battalion London Regiment

(Erase heading not required.)

Instructions regarding War Diaries and Intelligence Summaries are contained in F.S. Regs., Part II. and the Staff Manual respectively. Title pages will be prepared in manuscript.

Hour, Date, Place		Summary of Events and Information	Remarks and references to Appendices
BRAINTREE.	9/12/15	2.Lt. J.F. FLINT. appointed Asst Adjutant and Musketry Officer vice Capt Owen. Brigade Exercise.	WS
"	10/12/15.	Transfer of Capt. A.H. CRABBE to 2t. H.A.S. COTTOR to 3/23rd Batt. London Regiment, cancelled. - Outpost Scheme (cancelled bad weather)	WS
"	11/12/15.	1. Officer & 27 other Ranks of the 2/21st Batt. London Regiment (M. Gun Sectn) attached for Billets & Rations. 1. Officer & 22 other Ranks of the 2/22nd Batt. London Regiment (M. Gun Sectn) attached for Billets & Rations.	WS WS
"	12/12/15.	Interior Economy. Church Parade.	WS
"	13/12/15	Company Training.	WS
"	14/12/15	Company Training.	WS
"	15/12/15.	Brigade Tactical Scheme cancelled owing to bad weather. Capt. N.B. Fox returned to duty from Sick leave	WBF

Army Form C. 2118.

WAR DIARY
or
INTELLIGENCE SUMMARY. 2/23rd Battalion London Regiment.

(Erase heading not required.)

Instructions regarding War Diaries and Intelligence Summaries are contained in F.S. Regs., Part II. and the Staff Manual respectively. Title pages will be prepared in manuscript.

Hour, Date, Place		Summary of Events and Information	Remarks and references to Appendices
BRAINTREE.	16/12/15.	Battalion Route March with tactical precautions via BLACK NOTLEY & WITHAM returning via CHIPPINGHILL & CRESSING.	N.B.F.
"	17/12/15.	Outpost Scheme. Capt. A.H. CRABBE & 2/Lt. COTTON transferred to 3/23rd Lon. Regmt.	See Appendix II
"	18/12/15.	Interior Economy.	N.B.F.
"	19/12/15.	Church Parade.	N.B.F.
"	20/12/15.	Route March via BOCKING & STISTED.	N.B.F.
"	21/12/15.	Mobilization Scheme. 2/Lt. J. HOLMES proceeded on course.	N.B.F.
"	22/12/15.	Company Training	N.B.F.
"	23/12/15.	Inspection by Major General E.S. BULFIN. C.V.O. C.B. commanding 60th London Division.	N.B.F.

Army Form C. 2118.

WAR DIARY
or
INTELLIGENCE SUMMARY. 2/23rd Battalion London Regiment.
(Erase heading not required.)

Instructions regarding War Diaries and Intelligence Summaries are contained in F. S. Regs., Part II. and the Staff Manual respectively. Title pages will be prepared in manuscript.

Hour, Date, Place	Summary of Events and Information	Remarks and references to Appendices
BRAINTREE. 24/12/15	Interior Economy.	J.R.T.
" 25/12/15	"Christmas" Dinner to N.C.O's & men of the 2/23rd Batt. London Regt.	J.R.T.
" 26/12/15	Church Parade.	J.R.T.
" 27/12/15	Concentration March (cancelled owing to bad weather)	J.R.T.
" 28/12/15	Battalion Route March to BANNISTER GREEN via RAYNE and BLAKE END returning via MILCH HILL & YOUNGS END.	J.R.T.
" 29/12/15	Company Training. Rifle Inspection.	J.R.T.
" 30/12/15	Brigade Tactical Scheme 8.30 AM to 4 PM.	J.R.T.
" 31/12/15	Outpost Scheme at Gt SALING.	See Appendix III.

J. Truefitt Lt Col.
Commanding 2/23 London Regiment.

Appendix. I

TACTICAL EXERCISE.

2/23rd BATTALION, THE LONDON REGIMENT.
3rd December 1915.
_____

Report by Lieut-Col. H. Streatfeild
commanding.
----

1. SCHEME. Copy of Operation Orders, General Idea and
            Special Idea, and Instructions.

2. REMARKS.

Exercise was carried out satisfactorily. Owing to shortage of men supports were regarded as imaginary, but positions for them were selected & marked. Communication scheme carried out by signallers with flags as insufficient telephones were available. It was explained that flags would not be used under actual service conditions.

................Lieut-Col.
Comdg. 2/23rd Battn. The London Regt.

Braintree.

OPERATION ORDERS

by

LIEUT-COLONEL H. STREATFEILD
Commanding, 2/23rd Battalion, The London Regiment.

BRAINTREE   December 3rd 1915.

---

1. The Battalion will take up an outpost from E in DOVEWARDS HALL on the BOCKING-GOSFIELD ROAD inclusive, to points on 200 contour south of L in LYONS HALL.

2. The 2/24th Battalion, The London Regiment will continue the line to the left. Arrangements will be made for safeguarding the right flank.

3. Companies will occupy the section from left to right in the following order. "D" "C" "B" "A".   Company frontage will be allotted on the ground.

4. **AMMUNITION.** Pack animals will be unloaded at Company Headquarters, and withdrawn to a position in rear of the line. Battalion S.A.A. carts will be parked on side of BOCKING-GOSFIELD ROAD, west of Mill.

5. **DRESSING STATION.** FARM E of BOCKING-GOSFIELD ROAD, about 400 yards south of left of Section.

6. Reports to same station as "5".

                    (Signed) H. Streatfeild, Lt-Col.
                    Commdg. 2/23rd Battalion, London Regiment.

Issued at 7-30 a.m. by cyclist orderly.

Copy No. 1. to 2/24th Battn. London Regiment.
Copy No. 2. to O.C."A" Coy.   Copy No. 3. to O.C. "B" Coy.
Copy No. 4. to O.C."C" Coy.   Copy No. 5. to O.C. "D" Coy.
Copy No. 6. to Medical Officer.
Copy No. 7. to Signalling Officer.
Copy No. 8. to Machine Gun Officer.
Copy No. 9. to Transport Officer.

GENERAL IDEA.

An enemy force is advancing from the N.E. on CHELMSFORD.

The 60th Division has concentrated during the night of the 2/3rd November in and around BRAINTREE, with a view of resisting this advance on the line BOCKING, CHURCH STREET-SISTED. Enemy cavalry patrols have been engaged by our Cavalry at 6 a.m. on the 3rd inst. at SUDBURY.

SPECIAL IDEA.

The 181st Infantry Brigade have been detailed to furnish outposts for the somewhat exhausted remainder of the Division, resting in Braintree.   Sections allotted as follows.

24th Battalion from   to E in DOVEWARDS HALL on BOCKING GOSFIELD ROAD, exclusive.

23rd Battalion, from E in DOVEWARDS on BOCKING-GOSFIELD ROAD inclusive to point on 200 contour S of L on LYONS HALL.

21st and 22nd Battalion (imaginary) in reserve in N portion of BOCKING.

Outposts to be in position by 11 a.m. on the 3rd inst.

          (Signed) H. Streatfeild, Lt-Col.
        Commdg. 2/23rd Battn. London Regiment.

I N S T R U C T I O N S.

1. Owing to weak state of Battalion, for the purpose of the Exercise, Companies will be formed into two platoons and Company Commanders will regard their other two platoons (imaginary) as supports. The position of their supports should, however, be decided on by Company Commanders.

Officers Commanding Companies will provide themselves with string, and will tape out the trenches they would propose to dig.

Every man should be used for some duty in connection with the tactical portion of the scheme. Cooks, fatigue men etc., should be imaginary. Civilians will not be interfered with.

The Battalion Signallers will try to obtain details of our dispositions, and to get through the Battalion lines. It is to be noted that the foiling by concealment of the first object is as important as the capturing of the Signallers.

Officers Commanding Companies will meet the Commanding Officer at E in DOVEWARDS HALL at 9. a.m. on the 3rd inst.

(Signed) H.Streatfeild. Lt-Col.
Commdg. 2/23rd Battn. London Regt.

Appendix II

TACTICAL EXERCISE.

2/23rd BATTALION, THE LONDON REGIMENT.

17th December 1915.

Report by Lieut-Col. H. Streatfeild
commanding.

1. SCHEME.   Copy of Operation Orders, General Idea and Special Idea attached.

2. REMARKS. The exercise was carried out satisfactorily. Owing to the shortage of men every man was put in the piquet line, supports &c being regarded as imaginary. The positions of these latter being decided on & marked.

   Company sectors were not allotted in attached orders, owing to the impossibility of defining them on the small scale maps provided.

Lieut-Col.
Comdg. 2/23rd Battalion, The London Regiment.

OPERATION ORDERS.
by
LIEUT-COLONEL H. STREATFEILD.
COMMANDING 2/23rd BATTALION, THE LONDON REGIMENT.
BRAINTREE.   December 17th 1915.

---

1. The 181st Infantry Brigade will halt in the vicinity of the road junction N of H in MULSHAM HALL for rest and food.

   ---

2. Enemy advance guards have been reported at COGGESHALL, KELVEDON and WITHAM, and an enemy cavalry patrol has been seen by one of our cyclists at BLACK NOTLEY at 8-30 a.m. this morning.

   ---

3. The 2/23rd Battalion The London Regiment will furnish outposts for the protection of the Brigade while it is resting; the rear guard, the 2/24th Battalion The London Regiment (imaginary), will furnish a screen until the 2/23rd Battalion is in position.

   ---

4. Officers Commanding Companies, Machine Gun Officer and Signalling Officer will meet the Commanding Officer at cross roads S of Bushy Wood on BRAINTREE - CHELMSFORD ROAD at 10-30 p.m., when Company frontages will be allotted, and further orders issued.

(Signed) H. STREATFEILD, Lt-Col.

Condg. 2/23rd Battalion, The London Regiment.

Issued at 8-30 p.m.
     Copy No. 1. Headquarters, 181st Infantry Brigade.
     Copy No. 2. to O.C. "A" Company.
     Copy No. 3. to O.C. "B" Company.
     Copy No. 4. to O.C. "C" Company.
     Copy No. 5. to O.C. "D" Company.
     Copy No. 6. to Machine Gun Officer.
     Copy No. 7. to Signalling Officer.
     Copy No. 8. to Medical Officer.
     Copy No. 9. Filed.

GENERAL IDEA.

A White force is retiring from COLCHESTER in the direction of LONDON, and has succeeded in disengaging itself from an advancing Blue Force of superior numbers.

SPECIAL IDEA.

The 181st Infantry Brigade acting as a detached force to hinder the advance of the enemy has halted for a few hours in the vicinity of the road junction N of H in HULSHAM HILL, and the 23rd Battalion has been ordered to take up an outpost line for the protection of the remainder of the Brigade while it is altered.

(Signed) H. STREATFEILD, Lt-Col.
Comdg. 2/23rd Battalion, London Regt.

Appendix VII

TACTICAL EXERCISE

2//23rd BATTALION, THE LONDON REGIMENT.

31st December 1915.

Report by Lieut-Col. H. Streatfeild
commanding.

1. <u>SCHEME.</u> Copy of Operation Orders, General idea and Special idea attached.

2. <u>REMARKS.</u>

Verbal orders were issued on the ground as to dispositions &c. Heavy rain then came on, which in fact continued throughout the day. The exercise was therefore discontinued, & the battalion marched home.

H. Streatfeild
Lieut-Col.
Comdg. 2/23rd Battalion, The London Regiment.

ORDERS.

by

LIEUT-COLONEL H. STREATFEILD
COMMANDING 2/23rd BATTALION THE LONDON REGIMENT.

BRAINTREE.   December 30th 1915.

1. The 181st Infantry Brigade is halted in the vicinity of the road junction W of G in Great Saling for rest and food.

2. Enemy scouts have been seen by our scouts at Hawbush Green this morning at 9 a.m. and the enemy cyclists have been reported at White Notley.

3. The 2/23rd Battalion, The London Regiment will furnish outpost for the protection of the remainder of the Brigade while it is resting. The 2/24th Battalion, The London Regiment (imaginary) will furnish a screen until the 2/23rd Battalion, The London Regiment is in position.

4. Officers Commanding Companies and the Signalling Officer will meet the C.O. at road junction W. of G. in Great Saling at 10.30 a.m., when company frontages will be allotted and further orders issued.

(Signed) H. Streatfeild. Lt-Col.

Commdg. 2/23rd Battn, Lond. Rgt.

Issued by orderly at 6 p.m.

No.1. Copy 181st Infantry Brigade.
No.2. Copy O.C. "A" Coy.
No.3. Copy O.C. "B" Coy.
No.4. Copy O.C. "C" Coy.
No.5. Copy O.C. "D" Coy.
No.6. Copy. Signalling Officer
No.7. Copy Transport Officer.
No.8. Copy Filed.

GENERAL IDEA.

A Blue Force is advancing from Haldon in the direction
of Thaxted and has succedded in forcing the retiral
of an inferior White Force.

SPECIAL IDEA.

The 181st Infantry Brigade has halted in the vicinity
of the road junction W of G in Great Saling for food
and rest and the 2/23rd Battalion, The London Regiment
has been orderdd to take up an outpost line for the
protection of the remainder of the Brigade while it
is resting.

                           (Signed) H. Streatfeild. Lt-Col.
                           Commdg. 2/23rd Battn. The Lond. Regt.

www.ingramcontent.com/pod-product-compliance
Lightning Source LLC
Chambersburg PA
CBHW081507160426
43193CB00014B/2615